I0893119

Wilma Wilderness's Guide to... Birds

Written by
Charis Mather

KidHaven
PUBLISHING

Published in 2026 by
KidHaven Publishing, an Imprint of Greenhaven Publishing, LLC
2544 Clinton St., Buffalo, NY 14224

Written by: Charis Mather
Edited by: Rebecca Phillips-Bartlett
Designed by: Amelia Harris

Cataloging-in-Publication Data
Names: Mather, Charis, 1999-.
Title: Birds / Charis Mather.
Description: Buffalo, NY : KidHaven Publishing, 2026. | Series: Wilma Wilderness's guide to... | Includes glossary and index.
Identifiers: ISBN 9781534551497 (pbk.) | ISBN 9781534551503 (library bound) | ISBN 9781534551510 (ebook)
Subjects: LCSH: Birds--Juvenile literature. | Birds--Adaptations--Juvenile literature. | Birds--Behavior--Juvenile literature. | Birds--Habitat--Juvenile literature.
Classification: LCC QL676.2 M384 2026 | DDC 598--dc23

Printed in China

CPSIA compliance information: Batch #QW26KH: For further information contact Greenhaven Publishing LLC at 1-844-317-7404.

Please visit our website, www.greenhavenpublishing.com. For a free color catalog of all our high-quality books, call toll free 1-844-317-7404 or fax 1-844-317-7405.

Find us on

All images are courtesy of Shutterstock.com, unless otherwise stated.
Cover – Lauritta, Alex Cooper Photography, Independent birds, Dennis Jacobsen. Recurring – AlinArt, haru_natsu_kobo, Kobee. 2–3 – Geshas. 4–5 – Vibe Images, Natalia Paklina. 6–7 – Hioe Hendro, Martin Pelanek, PCH.Vector. 8–9 – Macrovector, L.A. Faille, Dani Jara. 10–11 – takmat71, Agami Photo Agency, Ondrej Prosicky. 12–13 – Rudmer Zwerver, PhotoJanski, Ondrej Prosicky. 14–15 – Andrew Mohamed, Harry Collins Photography, John Navajo, Pixelcrafts. 16–17 – Super Prin, CanadianTimber. 18–19 – Rumka vodki, Anna Kucherova, Michael Tatman, Albert Beukhof, Andrew M. Allport. 20–21 – SofiaV, DESPITE STRAIGHT LINES, Vee Snijders. 22–23 – Skamai, Alfmaler, PCH.Vector, Anelya93.

Contents

Words that look like **this** can be found in the glossary on page 24.

A Wilderness of Wonders

Welcome to Wilma Wilderness's Guide to Birds! I am Wilma. One of my favorite activities is going out in nature to explore. There are all kinds of creatures in the wild that are worth learning about.

This guide is all about birds. The wilderness is a great place to watch them in their natural habitat. Get ready to learn all about how birds live and what makes them so wonderful.

Why We Need Birds

Birds are very important to the planet. They have a big part to play in the food chain. Some birds help plants by eating their fruit and spreading their seeds to new places.

All birds are warm-blooded and have wings, feathers, and a backbone. However, birds in different habitats have different features and behaviors. To identify birds, it helps to pay attention to those differences.

Warm-blooded means having blood that stays at a steady, warm temperature.

Become a Birdwatcher

The best way to learn about birds is to watch them. Notice their shape, size, and colors. See whether their beaks are short or long, straight or curved. Look at their feet and legs.

Birds that live in water usually have webbed feet.

Feature Focus

When you see a bird, think about these things:

What color are its feathers?

Is it big or small?

Does it have any special features?

What shape are its feet and beak?

These grebes have long necks and spiked head feathers.

All Sorts of Appearances

What differences can you see between these birds?

Swifts are easy to identify from far away thanks to their banana-shaped wings.

Penguins have wings but cannot fly. Their flippers and webbed feet help them swim.

Flamingos get their pink color from the food they eat. They have long necks and legs.

The Life of Birds

Where birds live depends on what they need to survive. If birds eat fruits and seeds, they will live in places with lots of plant life. If they eat fish, they will live near water.

Feature Focus

These questions can help you identify birds:

All Sorts of Nests

Many weaver birds build hanging nests out of grass. Weavers usually eat insects or seeds.

Woodpeckers live in holes in tree trunks. They peck the tree bark to find bugs.

Cuckoos do not build their own nests. They lay their eggs in the nests of other birds so that they do not have to feed their own young.

Behavior

How birds sound, move, and act can tell you a lot about them. When you see a bird, don't just look at its physical features. Pay attention to its behavior, too.

Feature Focus

Ask these questions to help you find out more:

What sound does the bird make?

Is the bird active in the day or at night?

Is it alone or in a group?

How is the bird moving?

All Sorts of Activities

Some birds show off to find a mate. Some birds do this by dancing or spreading out their feathers. Male peacocks have very impressive feathers.

Birds often preen their feathers to keep clean. Some birds preen to make their feathers waterproof.

Many types of birds fly together in groups called flocks. This helps to keep them safe. Starlings sometimes gather into large, cloud-like flocks called murmurations.

Wonderfully Wild Birds

Crows might not seem like the most interesting birds from their physical features. However, these are some of the most intelligent animals out there. They are great at learning and remembering information.

Kiwi birds do have wings, but they are too small to see. This means they cannot fly. To find food, kiwi birds poke around the ground with their long beaks.

Wild kiwi birds are only found in New Zealand.

Get Exploring!

When in the wilderness, be on the lookout for birds. Even if you cannot see any, you may be able to hear them or see signs of them. Look out for their nests or tracks.

Why not keep a record of the birds you come across? In a notebook, write down what they look like, where you saw them, and what they were doing. Make your own wilderness guide!

Glossary

behaviors the ways living things act

environment the natural world, or something's natural surroundings

food chain the way living things depend on each other for food

habitat the natural home in which animals, plants, and other living things live

identify to find out what something is based on what someone knows about it

mate a partner of the same species that an animal produces young with

preen for a bird to use its beak to look after its feathers

webbed of feet that have toes that are connected by a thin bit of skin

Index